EXPLORING SCIENCE

THE PERIODIC TABLE

MAPPING THE ELEMENTS

BY SHARON KATZ COOPER

Content Adviser: Martin Feldman, Ph.D., Professor of Chemistry, Emeritus,
Howard University, Washington, D.C.

Science Adviser: Terrence E. Young Jr., M.Ed., M.L.S.,
Jefferson Parish (Louisiana) Public School System

Reading Adviser: Rosemary G. Palmer, Ph.D., Department of Literacy,
College of Education, Boise State University

 Compass Point Books · Minneapolis, Minnesota

Compass Point Books • 3109 West 50th Street, #115 • Minneapolis, MN 55410

Visit Compass Point Books on the Internet at *www.compasspointbooks.com*
or e-mail your request to *custserv@compasspointbooks.com*

Photographs ©: Tek Image/Photo Researchers, Inc., cover; Lester V. Bergman/Corbis, 4; Novosti/ Photo Researchers, Inc., 5; Kiyoshi Takahase Segundo/Shutterstock, 6; Michael Brown/Shutterstock, 10–11; Astrid & Hanns-Frieder Michler/Photo Researchers, Inc., 13; Lawrence Berkeley National Laboratory/Photo Researchers, Inc., 14; The Smithsonian Institute/AIP/Photo Researchers, Inc., 15; Rosenfeld Images Ltd/Photo Researchers, Inc., 16; Charles D. Winters/Photo Researchers, Inc., 17, 29, 35; AJPhoto/Photo Researchers, Inc., 19; BSIP/Photo Researchers, Inc., 20; Martyn F. Chillmaid/Photo Researchers, Inc., 21; John M. Daugherty/Photo Researchers, Inc., 22; Shigemi Numazawa/Atlas Photo Bank/Photo Researchers, Inc., 23; STR/epa/Corbis, 24; Michael Gilbert/Photo Researchers, Inc., 25; Andrew McClenaghan / Photo Researchers, Inc., 26; Nigel Cattlin/Photo Researchers, Inc., 27; Stephen & Donna O'Meara/Photo Researchers, Inc., 28; Brook / Photo Researchers, Inc, 30; David McCarthy/Photo Researchers, Inc., 31; Jonathan Blair/Corbis, 32; Ronnie Comeau/Istock Photo, 34; National Cancer Institute/Photo Researchers, Inc, 37; Narcisa Floricica Buzlea/Shutterstock, 38; Mary Evans Picture Library, 40; SPL/Photo Researchers, Inc., 41; Omikron/Photo Researchers, Inc., 42; Charles & Josette Lenars/Corbis, 44; Perennou Nuridsany/Photo Researchers, Inc., 46.

Editor: Anthony Wacholtz
Designer/Page Production: Bobbie Nuytten
Photo Researcher: Lori Bye
Illustrators: Ashlee Schultz and Farhana Hossain

Art Director: Jaime Martens
Creative Director: Keith Griffin
Editorial Director: Carol Jones
Managing Editor: Catherine Neitge

Library of Congress Cataloging-in-Publication Data
Cooper, Sharon Katz.
   The Periodic table : mapping the elements / by Sharon Katz Cooper.
      p. cm. — (Exploring science)
   Includes bibliographical references and index.
   ISBN-13: 978-0-7565-1961-2 (library binding)
   ISBN-10: 0-7565-1961-6 (library binding)
   ISBN-13: 978-0-7565-1967-4 (paperback)
   ISBN-10: 0-7565-1967-5 (paperback)
   1. Periodic law—Juvenile literature. 2. Chemical elements—Juvenile literature.
   I. Title. II. Series.
   QD467.C66 2006
   546'.8—dc22   2006027049

(About the Author)

Sharon Katz Cooper is a writer and science educator. She enjoys writing about science and social studies topics for children and young adults. She lives in Fairfax, Virginia, with her husband, Jason, and son, Reuven.

TABLE OF CONTENTS

CHAPTER ONE

Amazing Elements

IN 1875, FRENCH CHEMIST Paul Lecoq de Boisbaudran discovered the element gallium, a silver-colored metal. In 1878, Swedish chemist Lars Nilson discovered the element scandium in a couple of minerals that were thought to be unique to Scandinavia. And in 1886, German chemist Clemens Winkler discovered germanium, which he patriotically named for his country.

These pioneering chemists were proud to have found and named the new elements. The discoveries were significant contributions to science. However, Dimitri Mendeleev, a Russian chemist, had predicted their existence years before. In 1871, Mendeleev had published an early version of the periodic table, which he put together by playing

The melting point of gallium is 85.6 degrees Fahrenheit (29.8 degrees Celsius). The metal will begin to melt in the palm of a person's hand.

a form of "chemistry solitaire" with cards of the elements. He realized that the elements had certain things in common and could be arranged in groups. He also noticed that some of his groups were missing elements. Mendeleev was so confident about the arrangement of his groups that he boldly predicted the existence of the unknown elements. He even predicted how much they would weigh and how they would behave. As Lecoq de Boisbaudran, Nilson, and Winkler later found out, for the most part, Mendeleev was right.

WHAT IS AN ELEMENT?

Most objects are made of a combination of substances called elements. An element is a substance that cannot be broken down any further. For example, if you take apart a sofa, breaking it down into wood, nails, and cushions, you can still take apart the cushions and separate them into different kinds of

Dimitri Mendeleev (1834–1907) created the periodic table while he was a professor at the University of St. Petersburg in Russia.

fabrics. You can keep taking apart the pieces of the sofa and separating them into different materials. Eventually, when the substances cannot be broken down any further, you are left with elements.

Elements are made of particles called atoms. Inside an atom is a nucleus, which consists of protons and neutrons, and a swarm of electrons that circle around the nucleus, much as tiny planets orbit the sun. Each atom has a number of these orbits—known as shells—which extend farther and farther out from the nucleus.

Tiny electrons (red) orbit the nucleus of an atom.

The number of electrons in an atom's outer shell determines many of its properties. Electrons in the outer shell are farthest from the nucleus, and the nucleus' hold on them is weaker than the hold on the inner shells. Some electrons jump to a different atom or attract other electrons to their own orbit. These electrons easily react, or interact, with other atoms.

The atom's electrical charge determines whether electrons are gained or lost. Inside the atom, protons carry a positive electrical charge, and electrons carry a negative electrical charge. Neutrons have no charge. Normally, an atom has no

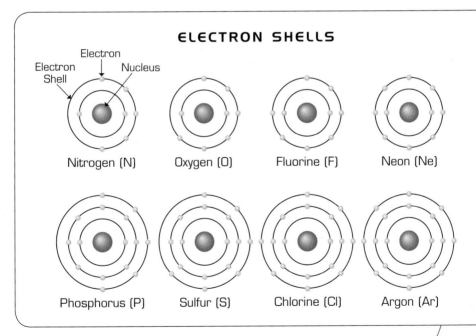

ELECTRON SHELLS

Electron
Electron | Nucleus
Electron Shell

Nitrogen (N)   Oxygen (O)   Fluorine (F)   Neon (Ne)

Phosphorus (P)   Sulfur (S)   Chlorine (Cl)   Argon (Ar)

Elements with the same number of electrons in their outer shell have similar properties.

electrical charge because it is evenly balanced by an equal number of protons and electrons. If an electron leaves or joins an atom, the atom obtains an electrical charge.

Any atom with an electrical charge is called an ion. An atom that loses an electron has a positive charge and is called a cation. An atom that gains an electron has a negative charge and is called an anion. Elements react with each other to balance their charges and fill their outermost electron shells. A cation attracts an anion to make a neutral compound.

Metals, for example, have few electrons in their outer shells, so they tend to lose them and form cations when they react. This means they are left with fewer shells, but they are

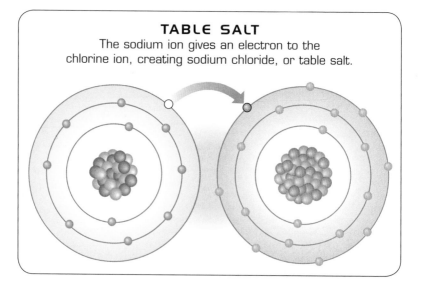

TABLE SALT
The sodium ion gives an electron to the chlorine ion, creating sodium chloride, or table salt.

all complete. Nonmetals, which tend to have more electrons in their outer shells, tend to attract electrons and form anions, thus filling their existing outer shells.

Mendeleev did not know about the structure of protons and electrons within atoms. He only knew the relative weights of the elements when they combined. For example, chemists knew that an atom of oxygen was 16 times as heavy as an atom of hydrogen, the lightest element. So if hydrogen was given a relative weight of 1, oxygen's relative weight would be 16.

These relative weights were called atomic weights, and we now know that atomic weights are based on the weights of the protons and neutrons in the nucleus (an electron's weight is very small). Mendeleev noticed that the elements had similar chemical behaviors after arranging the elements in order by atomic weight. However, it is actually the number of protons (or electrons) in an atom that determines how it behaves, not its weight. The number of protons in an element is known as its atomic number.

Mendeleev noticed similarities among the elements, and he grouped the similar elements in columns. We now understand his table in terms of the structure of atoms: For the most part, all the elements in one column have the same number of electrons in their outer shells. Together these elements are called a group. The resulting chart was named the periodic table.

The Periodic Table

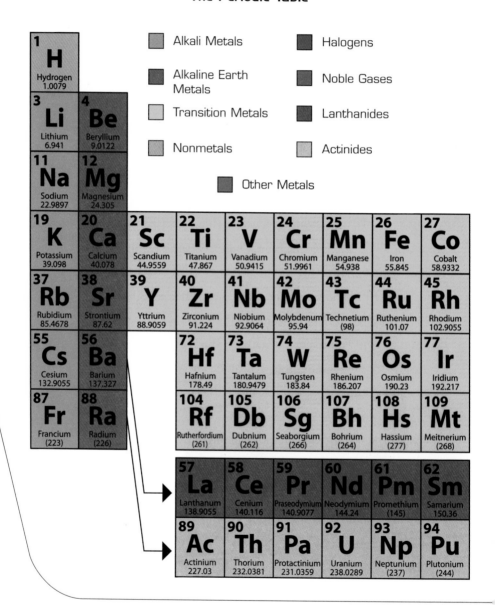

	Alkali Metals		Halogens
	Alkaline Earth Metals		Noble Gases
	Transition Metals		Lanthanides
	Nonmetals		Actinides
	Other Metals		

1
H
Hydrogen
1.0079

3
Li
Lithium
6.941

4
Be
Beryllium
9.0122

11
Na
Sodium
22.9897

12
Mg
Magnesium
24.305

19
K
Potassium
39.098

20
Ca
Calcium
40.078

21
Sc
Scandium
44.9559

22
Ti
Titanium
47.867

23
V
Vanadium
50.9415

24
Cr
Chromium
51.9961

25
Mn
Manganese
54.938

26
Fe
Iron
55.845

27
Co
Cobalt
58.9332

37
Rb
Rubidium
85.4678

38
Sr
Strontium
87.62

39
Y
Yttrium
88.9059

40
Zr
Zirconium
91.224

41
Nb
Niobium
92.9064

42
Mo
Molybdenum
95.94

43
Tc
Technetium
(98)

44
Ru
Ruthenium
101.07

45
Rh
Rhodium
102.9055

55
Cs
Cesium
132.9055

56
Ba
Barium
137.327

72
Hf
Hafnium
178.49

73
Ta
Tantalum
180.9479

74
W
Tungsten
183.84

75
Re
Rhenium
186.207

76
Os
Osmium
190.23

77
Ir
Iridium
192.217

87
Fr
Francium
(223)

88
Ra
Radium
(226)

104
Rf
Rutherfordium
(261)

105
Db
Dubnium
(262)

106
Sg
Seaborgium
(266)

107
Bh
Bohrium
(264)

108
Hs
Hassium
(277)

109
Mt
Meitnerium
(268)

57
La
Lanthanum
138.9055

58
Ce
Cenium
140.116

59
Pr
Praseodymium
140.9077

60
Nd
Neodymium
144.24

61
Pm
Promethium
(145)

62
Sm
Samarium
150.36

89
Ac
Actinium
227.03

90
Th
Thorium
232.0381

91
Pa
Protactinium
231.0359

92
U
Uranium
238.0289

93
Np
Neptunium
(237)

94
Pu
Plutonium
(244)

Scientists have discovered elements 112–116 and 118, but the atoms of these elements lasted a very short time. These elements, which were named after the Latin equivalent of their atomic number, are not recognized by the International Union of Pure and Applied Chemistry.

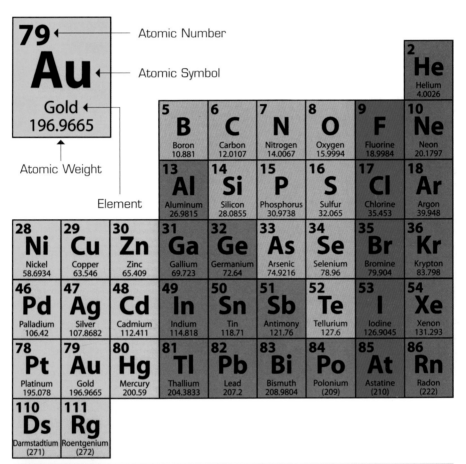

79 ← Atomic Number

Au ← Atomic Symbol

Gold ← Element

196.9665

↑ Atomic Weight

						2 **He** Helium 4.0026
5 **B** Boron 10.881	**6** **C** Carbon 12.0107	**7** **N** Nitrogen 14.0067	**8** **O** Oxygen 15.9994	**9** **F** Fluorine 18.9984	**10** **Ne** Neon 20.1797	
13 **Al** Aluminum 26.9815	**14** **Si** Silicon 28.0855	**15** **P** Phosphorus 30.9738	**16** **S** Sulfur 32.065	**17** **Cl** Chlorine 35.453	**18** **Ar** Argon 39.948	

28 **Ni** Nickel 58.6934	**29** **Cu** Copper 63.546	**30** **Zn** Zinc 65.409	**31** **Ga** Gallium 69.723	**32** **Ge** Germanium 72.64	**33** **As** Arsenic 74.9216	**34** **Se** Selenium 78.96	**35** **Br** Bromine 79.904	**36** **Kr** Krypton 83.798
46 **Pd** Palladium 106.42	**47** **Ag** Silver 107.8682	**48** **Cd** Cadmium 112.411	**49** **In** Indium 114.818	**50** **Sn** Tin 118.71	**51** **Sb** Antimony 121.76	**52** **Te** Tellurium 127.6	**53** **I** Iodine 126.9045	**54** **Xe** Xenon 131.293
78 **Pt** Platinum 195.078	**79** **Au** Gold 196.9665	**80** **Hg** Mercury 200.59	**81** **Tl** Thallium 204.3833	**82** **Pb** Lead 207.2	**83** **Bi** Bismuth 208.9804	**84** **Po** Polonium (209)	**85** **At** Astatine (210)	**86** **Rn** Radon (222)
110 **Ds** Darmstadtium (271)	**111** **Rg** Roentgenium (272)							

63 **Eu** Europium 151.964	**64** **Gd** Gadolinium 157.25	**65** **Tb** Terbium 158.9253	**66** **Dy** Dysprosium 162.5	**67** **Ho** Holmium 164.9303	**68** **Er** Erbium 167.259	**69** **Tm** Thulium 168.9342	**70** **Yb** Ytterbium 173.04	**71** **Lu** Lutetium 174.967
95 **Am** Americium (243)	**96** **Cm** Curium (247)	**97** **Bk** Berkelium (247)	**98** **Cf** Californium (251)	**99** **Es** Einsteinium (252)	**100** **Fm** Fermium (257)	**101** **Md** Mendelevium (258)	**102** **No** Nobelium (259)	**103** **Lr** Lawrencium (262)

Mendeleev's original periodic table helped future chemists to create a more modern version. Today the elements are listed by their atomic number. The periodic table organizes information about the elements into a format that is easy to understand.

Each element in the periodic table has a symbol and name. Each symbol is made of one or two letters. Some are obvious, such as H for hydrogen and O for oxygen. Some are less obvious, like Fe for iron. This symbol comes from the Latin word for iron, which is *ferrum*. Sometimes the names come from famous scientists (einsteinium), countries or cities where their discoverers lived (californium), or even planets in our solar system (neptunium).

The major groups of the periodic table are numbered left to right, from 1 to 18. The elements in group 1, or the first column, have one electron in their outer shells. These elements are highly reactive, which means they can lose their electron and combine easily with other elements. They are called soft or alkali metals. They include lithium, sodium, and potassium.

The elements in group 2 have two electrons in their outer shells. Skipping groups 3 through 12—they have varying numbers of electrons in their outer shells—the elements in group 13 have three electrons in their outer shells, the elements in group 14 have four electrons in their outer shells, and so on.

Since the elements in group 18 have eight electrons in their outer shells, it is full—this kind of shell can hold no more than eight electrons. Because this shell is full, these elements are almost completely nonreactive. This means they do not react with any other elements. These elements are called the noble gases.

All of the columns in the center of the periodic table (groups 3–12) make up the transition elements. The electrons in the transition elements are arranged in complicated ways and cause some unique properties in these elements, such as magnetism.

Potassium is a soft, highly reactive alkali metal.

Creating New Elements in the Lab

The last naturally occurring element is number 93, neptunium. So where did the rest come from? Scientists have artificially created them in a laboratory. They do this by fusing, or combining, the nuclei of smaller atoms to create an atom with a nucleus of a greater atomic weight.

For example, in 1994, scientists smashed together the 28 protons from nickel and the 82 protons from lead to get an element with 110 protons. This created element 110 on the periodic table—darmstadtium. However, they were only able to make a few atoms of this new element, and the atoms were so unstable that they quickly fell apart.

As recently as October 2006, scientists in California and Russia announced that they had created the heaviest known element— element 118. This new

Edwin Mattison McMillan (1907–1991) was awarded the 1951 Nobel Prize in chemistry for discovering neptunium.

element is called ununoctium (which is Latin for "one-one-eight") or eka-radon (beneath radon on the periodic table). In experiments that took more than 3,000 hours, scientists blasted billions of special calcium atoms at californium

atoms. Special sensors detected a total of three atoms of element 118 flying out of the mix. Each lasted about nine ten-thousandths of a second.

Though no one has discovered any practical uses of these heavy elements yet, scientists are hopeful that they will one day, especially if they can figure out how to make the atoms last a little longer. Scientists are optimistic about this, since it has happened before. For example, plutonium-239, a type of plutonium, was first created in the lab by scientists in 1941. It was then used as an essential ingredient in creating the first atomic bombs.

American physicist Glenn Seaborg (left) and Italian physicist Emilio Segre presented a sample of plutonium-239 to the Smithsonian Institution.

⊕ Metals

SCIENTISTS CLASSIFY a large number of elements as metals. Metals look shiny (or metallic), are good at transferring electricity and heat, are able to be manipulated into various shapes, and form cations. Metals can also be a combination of metallic elements. These are called alloys.

ALKALI METALS

The metals in group 1 of the periodic table are called alkali metals. They are silver-colored and have low melting points; this means they melt at relatively low temperatures, making them easy to work with. These metals' outer shells have one electron, which can easily jump to another kind of atom, making these elements highly reactive. They even react explosively with water. If pure potassium is

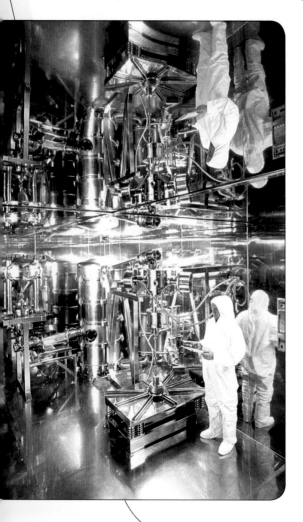

Alloys of titanium and steel are produced in a highly sanitary facility to avoid contamination. The composition of the alloys can be altered to maximize their strength, hardness, or other properties.

dropped in water, for example, it would fizz and bubble, giving off hydrogen gas. It would burn with a violet flame, and, because its melting point is so low, the heat of the reaction would cause it to melt and turn into a glob of liquid.

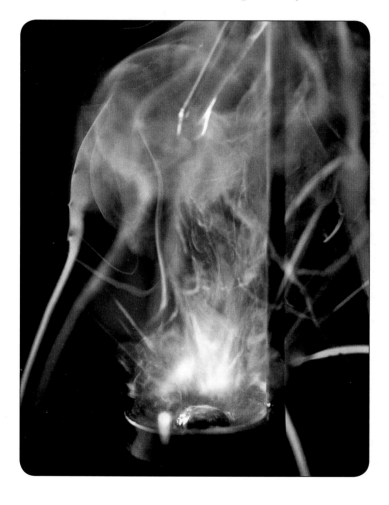

Potassium generates heat when exposed to water, creating an explosive reaction.

However, potassium and sodium do not exist in their pure forms in nature. They are far too reactive. Instead, there are thousands of compounds that contain these metals. One of the most common is sodium chloride, or table salt. We also find potassium chloride in Earth's oceans. The other elements in this group—such as lithium, rubidium, and cesium—are also found in many minerals in Earth's crust.

There are relatively few industrial uses for pure alkali metals because they are so reactive. Still, liquid sodium is sometimes used in nuclear reactors to help transfer heat. It is also used in the production processes of titanium, zirconium, and a few other metals.

On the other hand, compounds of the alkali metals are used in many ways. Sodium chloride is used to make many other sodium compounds, which are then used in manufacturing paper pulp, textiles, processed foods, leather, rubber, and glass, among other items.

Potassium compounds are widely used in fertilizers, and small amounts are used for matches, photographs, and glass. Lithium metal is used to make strong alloys with lead, aluminum, and other metals. These alloys are used in the manufacture of airplane parts and armor plating because they are so strong.

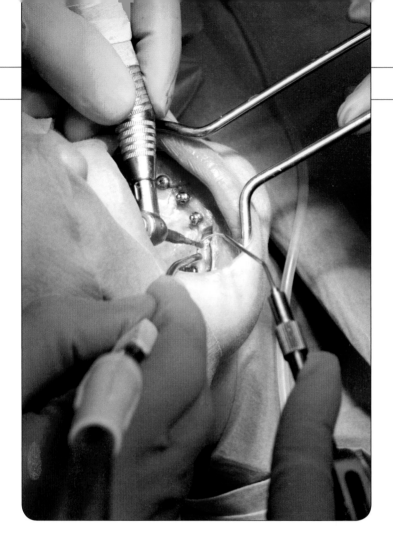

ALKALINE EARTH METALS

The elements in group 2 of the periodic table are the alkaline earth metals. These metals have two electrons in their outer shells, and most of them are grayish-white. They have a higher melting point than the alkali metals, making them stronger and more durable. They are found in Earth's crust, but because of their high reactivity, they are not found in their pure form.

Dentists use titanium screws as a replacement for the root of a tooth. Once in place, the screws bond directly to the jawbone.

Instead, they are mixed with rocks and minerals.

There are six alkaline earth metals—beryllium, magnesium, calcium, strontium, barium, and radium. Beryllium is used in X-rays to filter out the visible light rays and only allow X-rays to appear on the print. Because of its ability to absorb and reflect neutrons, it can also be used as a shield in nuclear reactors.

Scientists have been able to extract massive amounts of magnesium from seawater. When it is burned, it produces an extremely bright light. Therefore, it is used in flares and pho-

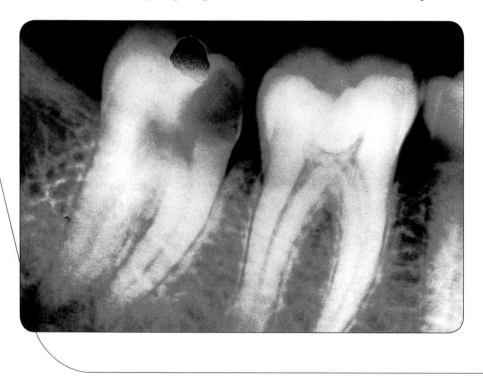

Berrylium filters out unnecessary light rays in X-rays so doctors can see the image in fine detail.

tographic flashbulbs. It is frequently made into an alloy with aluminum. This alloy is durable but light in weight, making it useful in airplanes, cameras, baseball catchers' masks, and other products.

Calcium is the fifth-most abundant element in Earth's crust. It is essential in humans—it strengthens teeth and bones and helps to regulate the heartbeat. Calcium can also be used

Magnesium can react with hydrochloric acid to generate hydrogen gas.

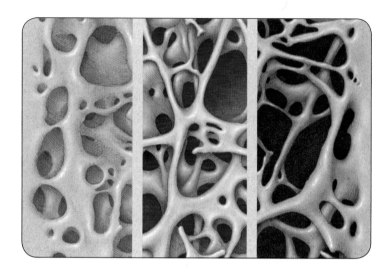

in compounds to create cement, fertilizers, and insecticides.

Strontium is softer than calcium and can be used in making the picture tubes in color television sets. It can also combine with iron to make magnets.

The word barium comes from the Greek word *barys*, meaning "heavy." Barium can be mixed with nickel to create an alloy used in spark plugs. The compound barium chloride is used as a water softener.

The main use for radium is to produce radon, a radioactive noble gas used to treat some types of cancer. Radium compounds were once used in luminous paint for aircraft instrument dials and the hands and numbers in a watch. However, since radium is highly radioactive, it was replaced by cobalt.

Osteoporosis is a condition caused by a lack of calcium, resulting in a decrease in bone density.

TRANSITION METALS

The groups in the middle of the periodic table are called the transition metals and inner transition metals. They are stronger than the alkali metals and less reactive. These include titanium, iron, nickel, copper, silver, and gold. These metals have been used by humans for thousands of years to make tools, weapons, utensils, and vehicles.

The lanthanides and actinides are located in two rows at the bottom of the periodic table. They are called rare earth ele-

Compounds of radium were once used in "glow in the dark" paint for the dials of aircraft equipment so pilots could read the dials in the dark.

ments, even though they are not especially rare. These shiny gray elements have almost the same chemical properties: They are good conductors of electricity, lose their shine easily, and occur naturally in minerals in the earth. They include some highly radioactive metals, such as uranium and thorium. Radioactive elements lose particles from their nuclei, eventually becoming another kind of atom. For example, uranium loses protons and neutrons to become lead.

Copper can be melted and molded into a different shape in a foundry.

CHAPTER THREE

NONMETALS—INCLUDING THE halogens and noble gases—make up 22 elements in the periodic table. These elements include some of the most familiar elements and those that are essential to our bodies and to life on Earth. They include oxygen, carbon, nitrogen, phosphorus, and sulfur.

Oxygen is the most abundant element on Earth. It makes up about 46 percent of the weight of Earth's crust, where it combines with other elements. It also makes up 20 percent of the atmosphere, where it exists as oxygen molecules—two oxygen atoms joined together. Oxygen also can be found as a highly reactive molecule containing three oxygen atoms, called ozone, which is formed in the stratosphere high above Earth. Stratospheric ozone forms a protective layer in the atmosphere that blocks out many UV-B rays—a type of sunlight that can be harmful to humans, animals, and plants.

A hole has developed in the ozone layer because of an excess of various pollutants.

Carbon is a unique element. It has four electrons in its outer shell, and its atoms combine with each other in nearly endless ways. As a result, we find carbon in nature in many forms. For example, the hard crystal we know as a diamond is a form of carbon, as is a soft black material known as graphite and a black solid material without crystals known as charcoal.

Carbon occurs both as a pure element and in combinations with many other elements. Carbon dioxide, a compound of carbon and oxygen, makes the survival of all green plants possible and, as a result, all life on Earth. In fact, organic compounds—those that contain carbon—make up about

Graphite, a form of carbon, is often used in pencils.

90 percent of all compounds known to scientists.

Nitrogen is one of the most common elements on Earth. It is a colorless and odorless gas. It makes up about 78 percent of the air we breathe. Nitrogen is found in proteins and nucleic acids, the principal components of living organisms. Compounds of nitrogen are used in foods, poisons, fertilizers, and explosives. Liquid nitrogen is often used to keep foods cold during storage and transportation.

Phosphorus is a waxy solid that is odorless and transparent, or see-through. In its rare, pure form, it will burn spontaneously in air. However, it is usually found in rocks, where it is mixed

An inorganic agricultural fertilizer known as NPK has a nitrogen base.

with other minerals. Phosphorus is highly toxic and must be handled carefully when it is used in industry. It is a common ingredient in fertilizers and used worldwide in agriculture. It is also part of monocalcium phosphate, which is in common baking powder. It is extremely important to human life; phosphorus is present in human cells, nerve tissue, and bones.

Sulfur is found in and around volcanoes, hot springs, and many kinds of mineral rocks. It is also found on meteorites. In its pure form, it is a hard yellow solid with no natural odor. It is widely used in gunpowder and fertilizers, and it can be used in paper manufacturing. It is also essential to life. It is a part of the body's proteins, fluids, and bone structure.

The elements in the second-to-last column in the periodic table (group 17) are called halogens. These include fluorine, chlorine, bromine, iodine, and astatine. They change from gas to liquid to unstable crystals as their atomic weight increases

A noxious gas poured out of the ground as sulfur deposits accumulated at the edges of a crack.

down the column. Fluorine and chlorine are highly reactive poisonous gases.
Bromine is a dark red liquid, iodine
is a gray solid, and astatine is very
unstable and extremely rare. They all
exist as diatomic (two-atom) molecules,
whether they are gases, liquids, or sol-
ids. This happens because they all have
seven electrons in their outermost shell.
When they share an electron as a pair,
they fill up that outermost shell and
achieve the stability of a filled shell.

Halogens are highly reactive, so they
are not generally found in a pure state in
nature. However, there are many compounds of halogens. For
example, hydrofluoric acid is used in making lightbulbs, and
aluminum chloride, a compound of aluminum and chlorine, is
commonly used as an antiperspirant.

DID YOU KNOW?

Astatine is the rarest of all naturally occurring elements. Scientists think there are only about 25 grams (0.875 ounces) on
the entire planet.

The word *bromine* is derived from the Greek *bromos*, which means "stench."

Industrial Uses of Nonmetals

Nonmetals have many uses in manufacturing. Fluorine is used in the production of a gas called sulfur hexafluoride. This gas is colorless, odorless, tasteless, stable, nontoxic, non-flammable, and nonreactive, so it is used as an insulator in electrical equipment.

Scientists and engineers convert sulfur into sulfur dioxide, which they use to make sulfuric acid. Workers combine it with

Sulfuric acid is the most widely used industrial chemical in the world.

other chemicals to make things like gasoline, plastics, medicines, pesticides, and tires. Two other examples are chlorine and nitrogen. Chlorine is widely used as a disinfectant, especially in swimming pools. Compounds of nitrogen are widely used in fertilizers, explosives, and artificial fibers.

Since organic compounds make up most of the compounds on Earth, they can be used in thousands of ways. Diamonds are the hardest substance known to humans, and many workers use diamond-coated drills to polish, grind, and cut other materials. Graphite is used to make pencils and lubricants. Plastics are organic compounds that were invented in 1909. There are now thousands of types of plastics. They are found in packaging, bottles, insulation, CDs, toys, glass substitutes, and many other products we use every day.

The diamond-coated tip of a dentist's drill can easily wear away tooth enamel during dental procedures.

Noble Gases

WHEN MENDELEEV DEVELOPED his periodic table, there was no column for the noble gases. None of them had yet been discovered. Today these elements—helium, neon, argon, krypton, xenon, and radon—form the last column of the periodic table. They are colorless and odorless gases. Unlike most other elements, they were once thought to be chemically inert, meaning that they do

An argon laser can produce many wavelengths simultaneously, which can be used to make holograms.

DID YOU KNOW?

The sun is largely made of helium. In fact, its name comes from *helios*, the Greek word for *sun.*

not react with anything else to form compounds. They do not even react with themselves to make molecules of more than one atom. Although they have since been found to react with a few other elements in laboratory experiments, they are highly nonreactive, and scientists have found no compounds of these gases in nature.

Why don't the noble gases react more often with other elements? Because their outermost electron shell is full. The shell contains eight electrons, and that is all it can hold. This makes them very stable. In other words, they do not "need" any other elements' electrons to make them stable.

Many uses for the noble gases have been discovered over the years. While oxygen is the most abundant element on Earth, hydrogen and helium are the most common elements in the universe. The mixture of hydrogen and helium supplies energy for hydrogen bombs. Deep-sea divers use a mixture of helium and oxygen to breathe when they are working under pressure. Various combinations of helium and oxygen are used, depending on how deep a diver is operating.

Most people are familiar with neon gas. In a vacuum tube, neon gas glows bright reddish orange when an electric current passes through it. As a result, it has been widely used for many years in advertising and store signage and in decorative lights. It is also used as a coolant and in the tubes of television sets.

Argon gas makes up less than 1 percent of the atmosphere. Libraries sometimes use argon to store historical documents to prevent them from decaying. Argon is also used in lightbulbs

When a party balloon is filled with helium, the balloon will float. Helium is also used in weather balloons and blimps because it is light and nonflammable.

because it will not react when heated by the filament inside.

Small amounts of krypton are in Earth's atmosphere, and traces have been found in Mars' atmosphere as well. Although colorless, krypton glows a magnificent white when stimulated by an electric charge.

Xenon is most commonly known for its use in strobe lights. Xenon lamps can also be used to kill bacteria. Xenon can form compounds with oxygen to create xenon trioxide, a highly explosive gas.

Radon is the heaviest known gas, and it turns yellow when the temperature drops. As the temperature decreases even further, it turns red-orange. Radon is present in some spring-waters, but it can be dangerous to humans if it is inhaled.

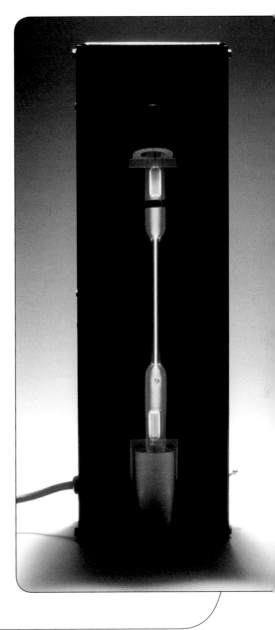

Xenon emits a blue light in a vacuum tube.

Radon Detectors

Radon forms from the decay of radium and uranium in soil. From there, radon can seep into houses from below. The amount of radon in the soil depends on the soil's chemistry. If there are deposits of radium or uranium under the house—usually found in rocks such as granites, shale, and coal beds—radon gas will form over time.

The amount of radon that rises into the house depends on the weather, the kind of soil, and the number of places in the house where the gas can enter. When there is warm air in the house, it rises and leaks out of openings around the roof and windows. This action creates a small amount of suction at the lower levels of the house. This suction can pull radon gas from the soil into the house.

Scientists have found that long-term exposure to high levels of radon can greatly increase a person's risk of developing lung cancer. As a result of this risk, the U.S. Environmental Protection Agency recommends that people test the air in their homes to check radon levels. This can be done with a test kit that contains a small amount of charcoal. The kit is left out in the lowest part of the house for several days. The charcoal absorbs radon gas in the air. After a few days, the kit is sealed and sent to a laboratory. There scientists can measure how much radon was absorbed. Since radon levels are usually

highest during the winter, scientists recommend testing at that time.

If a first test shows high levels of radon, officials will recommend doing several more tests or running more detailed tests. Homeowners can hire specially trained technicians to seal cracks in basement walls and floors, which should significantly lower the radon levels in the house.

Radon dectectors monitor the level of radon that accumulates in an enclosed or poorly ventilated area.

⊕ The History of the Periodic Table

THE ANCIENT GREEKS were among the first to think about what things are made of. Their "periodic table" only contained four elements—air, earth, fire, and water. In the sixth century B.C., the Greek philosopher Anaximander was the first person to propose these as the four fundamental elements that made up everything else. Anaximander argued that these four elements matched with four opposites: dry, cold, hot, and moist. Some philosophers around the same time thought that one of the four elements must be the one true fundamental element. They believed that everything must stem from just one

Air, earth, fire, and water were considered to be the first "elements" by the ancient Greeks.

kind of matter. Some thought it was water, some thought it was air, and some thought it was fire.

Aristotle, who lived two centuries after Anaximander, was a famous and well-respected Greek philosopher, and he was the first to develop a scientific method. He also believed that there were four elements, but he thought the elements were hot, cold, moist, and dry. Together, his elements made what he called four simple bodies. These bodies—fire, air, water, and earth—were the same as the fundamental elements of Anaximander, but Aristotle took it one step further. He thought each body was made of two elements. Air, for example, was made of hot and moist, and fire was made of hot and dry. Aristotle believed that everything on Earth was made of a combination of these bodies. For example, he knew of seven metals in his time—including gold, silver, and copper—but he did not think they were elements. In his view, they were somehow made from his four elements.

THE BIRTH OF MODERN CHEMISTRY

Anaximander's and Aristotle's ideas were believed for many hundreds of years. However, it wasn't until someone turned to the study of gases that true chemistry was born. Until someone realized that "air" was not simply one thing—that it was made of many kinds of substances—people could understand little about the way materials interacted with and were related to each other.

Belgian chemist Johann Baptista van Helmont discovered gases in the early 1600s by burning a weighed amount of charcoal. After it finished burning, only a small amount of ash remained. But when Helmont repeated the experiment inside a container, he discovered chemically produced gases when the escaping gas exploded the container.

The first element discovered—phosphorus—was chemically isolated in 1669. Over the next 200 years, excited chemists discovered many more elements. By 1869, there were

The ideas of Greek philosopher Aristotle contributed greatly to the field of science.

Light-bearing Phosphorus

German alchemist Hennig Brand became the first person to scientifically isolate a pure element when he discovered phosphorus in 1669. He found it by boiling urine until he saw fumes and liquid dripping out of what was left. He used more than 1,316 gallons (5,000 liters) of urine, which he produced himself, to isolate just a few ounces of the leftover liquid. When the liquid solidified, it gave off a pale, green glow. This was phosphorus, which comes from the Greek word meaning "light-bearing." Though Brand had been looking for a way to turn lead into gold, the discovery of phosphorus brought him a bit of fame and fortune anyway.

Alchemists, scientists who tried to turn common elements into gold, used symbols to represent their version of the elements.

about 63 known elements. These elements were different from each other in important ways, and chemists were interested in what made them different. English chemist John Dalton proposed in 1803 that each element was made of atoms, which he defined as small indestructible particles. He argued that elements vary because they have different atomic weights. This was the first move toward a modern atomic view of chemistry.

Scientists tried to organize the elements into groups. First they noticed groups of three. They saw that within certain groups of elements, one had an atomic weight that was halfway between the other two. Chlorine (17), bromine (35), and iodine (53) made a group like this. This was a good start, but it was incomplete.

Although earlier discoveries contributed to its development, Mendeleev is credited with the original periodic table.

John Dalton (1766–1844) was one of the founders of the modern atomic theory.

> **DID YOU KNOW?**
>
> In 1906, Mendeleev came within one vote of receiving the Nobel Prize in chemistry.

While working on a chemistry textbook, he wrote every element on a small card and arranged them in order of atomic weight. While doing this, he noticed that similar chemical properties occurred in a periodic way, at regular intervals. He began grouping them on his desk in columns based on these similar properties. What emerged in front of him was the first version of the modern periodic table.

He noticed that some elements were out of place, meaning that their properties matched better with the elements in a different column or row. Moving the elements to new places, he realized that many of the atomic weights were incorrect because of a lack of an accurate measuring device.

He also realized that there were holes in the table—places where an element of a certain atomic weight should fit, but none had yet been discovered. He predicted that elements would someday be discovered to fit in those slots. He was quite accurate: Seven of the 10 elements he predicted were later discovered. He published his table in 1869 and revised it in 1871. The modern periodic table was born.

ORGANIZING THE ELEMENTS

From left to right and from top to bottom, the periodic table is a thorough catalog of the elements that make up our planet and the universe. The table makes it possible to analyze all of the elements at once. It also provides basic information about each element in a format that is easy to understand. Although there is a lot more to chemistry than the periodic table, it is hard to imagine modern chemistry without it.

The Atomium, a structure representing an iron molecule, was built for the 1958 Brussels World's Fair.

alloy—combination of two or more metals

anion—negatively charged atom

atom—the smallest particle of an element

atomic number—the number assigned to an atom based on how many protons it has in its nucleus

atomic weight—the combined weight of an atom's protons and neutrons

cation—positively charged ion

electrons—tiny, negatively charged particles in an atom

element—substance that cannot be broken down into simpler substances

ion—atom with a positive or negative charge

neutrons—particles in the nucleus of an atom that have no charge

nucleus—the central part of an atom, containing neutrons and protons

organic compound—compound that contains carbon

protons—particles in the nucleus of an atom with a positive charge

radioactive—emitting particles from the nucleus of an atom

reactive—interacting with other atoms by gaining or losing electrons

▸ German chemist Julius Lothar Meyer (1830–1895) developed a periodic table similar to Mendeleev's—even though he worked completely independent of him—in 1868. Mendeleev got the credit, though, because he published his version first.

▸ Mendeleev was born in Siberia and was the youngest of 17 children.

▸ New Zealand physicist Ernest Rutherford discovered the nucleus of the atom in 1911.

▸ Hydrogen is the simplest atom. It has just one proton and one electron. It is the most abundant element in the universe. However, there is very little hydrogen in Earth's atmosphere because it is so light that Earth's gravity cannot keep it here.

▸ Silicon is the second-most abundant element on Earth. Compounds of silicon make up most of Earth's rock, sand, and soil.

▸ Iodine is a dark-colored solid. It was discovered when a scientist saw a purple gas coming from seaweed he had put in acid.

▸ Gold is one of the most precious metals known to humans. It has been used for money and trade for thousands of years. Its chemical symbol, Au, comes from the Latin *aurum*, which means "shining dawn."

▸ The first periodic table organized the elements in the shape of a cylinder, arranging them by increasing atomic weight. It was published in 1862.

Iodine gives off a purple gas when it is heated.

At the Library

Gray, Leon. *Iodine*. New York: Benchmark Books, 2005.

Miller, Ron. *The Elements*. Minneapolis: Twenty-First Century Books, 2006.

Oxlade, Chris. *Elements and Compounds*. Chicago: Heinemann Library, 2002.

Zannos, Susan. *Dmitri Mendeleyev and the Periodic Table*. Hockessin, Del.: Mitchell Lane Publishers, 2005.

On the Web

For more information on this topic, use FactHound.
1. Go to *www.facthound.com*
2. Type in this book ID: 0756519616
3. Click on the *Fetch It* button.
FactHound will find the best Web sites for you.

On the Road

New York Hall of Science
4701 111th St.
Queens, NY 11368
718/699-0005

The Franklin Institute Science Museum
222 N. 20th St.
Philadelphia, PA 19103
215/448-1200

Explore all the Physical Science books:

Atoms & Molecules: Building Blocks of the Universe

Chemical Change: From Fireworks to Rust

Manipulating Light: Reflection, Refraction, and Absorption

The Periodic Table: Mapping the Elements

Physical Change: Reshaping Matter

Waves: Energy on the Move

A complete list of Exploring Science titles is available on our Web site: *www.compasspointbooks.com*

INDEX